THE BOYS FROM SYRACUSE

VOCAL SELECTION

Music by

RICHARD RODGERS

Words by

LORENZ HART

Contents

© chappell/intersong ⊕

music group—usa

Exclusively Distributed By

HAL•LEONARD®
CORPORATION

7777 W. BLUEMOUND RD. P.O. BOX 13819 MILWAUKEE, WI 53213

Falling In Love With Love

Words by
LORENZ HART

Music by
RICHARD RODGERS

I weave with bright-ly col-ored strings To keep my mind off oth-er things; So, la-dies, let your fin-gers

Oh, Diogenes!

Words by
LORENZ HART

Music by
RICHARD RODGERS

The Shortest Day Of The Year

Words by
LORENZ HART

Music by
RICHARD RODGERS

✱Names of chords for Ukulele and Banjo.
Symbols for Guitar.

you._____ The small-est smile on your face Is the

great-est kind of em - brace. And a sin-gle kiss is a

thou-sand dreams come true._____ Your soft - est

sigh that is my strong - est tie. There's you, there's

Sing For Your Supper

Words by
LORENZ HART

Music by
RICHARD RODGERS

Hawks and crows do lots of things, But the ca - na - ry on - ly sings.

She is a cour - te - san on wings, So I've heard.

Ea - gles and storks are twice as strong, All the ca - na - ry knows is song,

But the ca - na - ry gets a - long, Gild - ed bird!

poco rit

Refrain *(not fast)*

Sing for your sup - per And you'll get break - fast, Song-birds al - ways.

p *a tempo*

eat If their song is sweet to hear.

Sing for your lunch - eon And you'll get din - ner, Dine with wine of choice If ro - mance is in your voice.

I heard from a wise ca - na - ry, Trill-ing makes a fel - low will - ing; So, lit - tle swal - low, swal - low now.

This Can't Be Love

Words by
LORENZ HART

Music by
RICHARD RODGERS

You Have Cast Your Shadow On The Sea

Words by
LORENZ HART

Music by
RICHARD RODGERS

Refrain
(slowly, with expression)

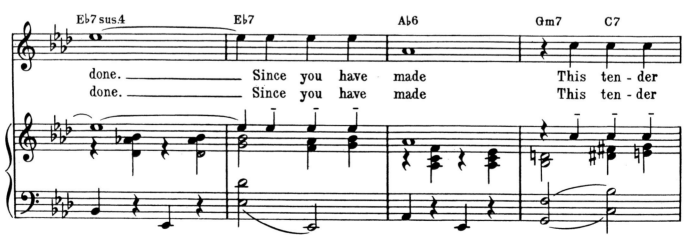